C000068364

WAL
EXMOOR

Twenty Country Walks
Within The Exmoor National Park

*Countryside Books' walking guides cover most areas of England and Wales
and include the following series:*

County Rambles
Walks for Motorists
Exploring Long Distance Paths
Literary Walks
Pub Walks

A complete list is available from the publishers:

3 Catherine Road, Newbury, Berkshire

WALKS IN EXMOOR

Twenty Country Walks
Within The Exmoor National Park

Christina Green

———————

COUNTRYSIDE BOOKS
NEWBURY, BERKSHIRE

First published 1981
by Spurbooks

This completely revised and updated edition
published 1992

COUNTRYSIDE BOOKS
3 Catherine Road
Newbury, Berkshire

ISBN 1 85306 161 1

Cover photograph: Lynton and Lynmouth from Countisbury Hill
taken by Bill Meadows

Publishers' Note

At the time of publication all footpaths used in these walks were
designated as official footpaths or rights of way, but it should be borne in
mind that diversion orders may be made from time to time.

Although every care has been taken in the preparation of this Guide,
neither the Author nor the Publisher can accept responsibility for those
who stray from the Rights of Way.

Typeset by Acorn Bookwork, Salisbury, Wiltshire
Produced through MRM Associates Ltd., Reading
Printed in England by J.W. Arrowsmith Ltd., Bristol

Acknowledgement

I wish to acknowledge the help of the Exmoor National Park Authority for information with waymarked walks, and the following authors, whose books have given me so much fascinating historial and topographical detail.

A Little History Of Exmoor, Hope Bourne, Dent, 1968
Portrait Of Exmoor, JHB Peel, Hale, 1970
Exmoor, Laurence Meynell, (The Regional Books Series), Hale, 1953
Exmoor, SH Burton, Hale, 1969
Exmoor Handbook And Gazetteer, NV Allen, The Exmoor Press, 1973

Contents

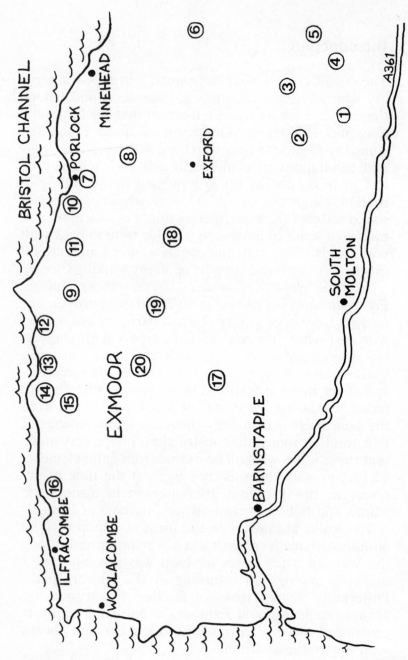

Sketch map showing locations of the walks

Introduction

These walks on Exmoor were small journeys of discovery which brought me immense pleasure, and I hope they will convey to others a touch of that same stimulation and enjoyment. On many of them I had the company of good friends who bore with me all the trials and tribulations of exploration and research; getting lost in bogs, ending up in ploughed fields, falling in brambles and slipping off stepping stones . . . To seasoned walkers these are merely minor distractions, but even so a sense of humour is a handy item to pack with your sandwiches, map and compass, and I am grateful for the tolerance and support of all my walking friends.

As time passes, of course, circumstances change. Footpath signs get turned around and even broken off; farmers have been known to erect barricades of barbed wire just where the age-old path enters their choicest bit of land; unfriendly dogs bark and harass on pack-horse routes through farmyards; man-made reservoirs spring up in once fertile valleys; groups of trees are felled, confusing the layout of forest paths; and even the land itself occasionally throws up new patches of bog, mud, or some other obstruction. I hope very much that these walks will still be as free from entanglements when you walk them as they were at the time of my research, but I cannot guarantee them against the whims and foibles of land-owners, farmers or Nature.

The walks are mostly in the form of a loop with an additional, smaller loop tacked on somewhere along the way. In a few cases no loop was possible, but I make no apology for returning by the outward path. Differently slanted views of familiar countryside are always fascinating and Exmoor, in particular, with its contrasted charms, has much to offer that isn't always seen the first time around.

Christina Green
March 1992

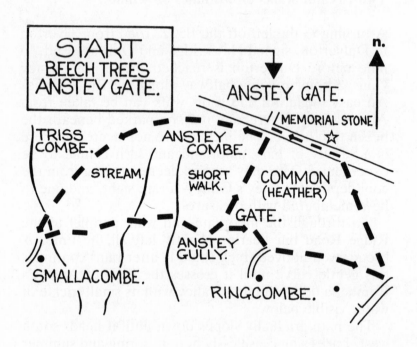

Anstey Gate

Two circular walks of 2¾ miles or 4 miles.

A turning to the left off the B3222 road from Tiverton to Dulverton, signed Hawkridge and Oldways End, ½ mile before Dulverton is reached, heads for Anstey Gate, a point roughly halfway along the Ridge Road. An easy, beautiful and short walk can be taken from Anstey Gate, where cars may be parked beneath the beech tree hedge. The inclines are not steep and there is a variety of bare moorland and lush combe to be experienced. You may see red deer emerging from the cool depth of Anstey's Gully – a rare sight, and one to be remembered with pleasure.

Go through the moorgate and walk parallel to the Ridge Road but bearing slightly left all the time. A broad, well-hooved track (muddy after rain) continues this gentle curve until it crosses the head of Anstey's Combe, a delightful little valley with its small trickle of water visible below.

The path gradually slopes down until it heads south west. Larks sing ceaselessly here in spring and summer and buzzards sail over the heathery hunting-ground all around. Even in hot weather the wind is ever-present and noisy. Sheep paths criss-cross and although you may catch distant sounds of farm dogs and tractors, the solitude is emphatic.

Turn left this side of a beech hedge that protects the Smallacombe enclosures and follow the track down through the gorse to the green shade of Anstey's Gulley

11

– a haven in spring, yet the precipitous sides of the gulley underline the force and fullness of Exmoor torrents in wintertime. Cross the water and follow the stony path upwards, noticing the impenetrable barrier of dry stone wall upon which beech saplings are laid. Beech tree windbreaks were planted on Exmoor during the middle of the 19th century, and will be seen frequently throughout this series of walks.

A clear track sweeps around beside the field hedges; the longer walk (4 miles) goes via this track, but there is a left hand cut-off path climbing towards the line of beech hedge and the Ridge Road at Anstey Gate, making the shorter loop a mere 2¾ miles.

For the longer walk, continue on over the cattle grid, passing the bridlepath sign to Molland – the way we have come – and following the track past the entrance to Ringcombe, where it becomes a metalled road.

At any point along this quiet little byway you could, if you wish, strike up through the heather, across West Anstey Common to the left, soon rejoining the Bridge Road. By turning left again you return to Anstey Gate.

If the longer route is followed, turn left on to a diagonal track clearly branching off the road, as it reaches the crest of a gentle hill, some ½ mile after Ringcombe entrance. On the right of the road here, a typical Exmoor gulley runs deep and green, fed by streams rising on the moorland above.

This path crosses Guphill Common and, keeping to the right hand fork halfway up the Common, joins the Ridge Road opposite a slate stone. This marks the boundary of the moorland memorial to P. Froude Hancock, a famous local staghunter. The granite stone – standing to the left, just off the road on the way back to Anstey Gate – weighs 13 tons and was erected in 1935, having been subscribed for by over 500 of Hancock's friends. It is the most recent in a line of memorial stones up here on the Ridge Road; not far away West Anstey Barrows can be seen on the skyline, burial places and memorials of Bronze Age chieftains, renowned in their own times as Hancock was in his.

The views from here are panoramic, with many landmarks to be picked out.

START
NR. CHURCH
HAWKRIDGE

HAWKRIDGE.

HOLLOWCOMBE
FARM.

ZEAL
FARM.

DANES
BROOK.

GREAT

COMMON.

n.

LONGER
WALK.

WEST
ANSTEY
BARROWS.

VENFORD.

Hawkridge

Two circular walks of 3½ miles and/or 2 miles.

Turn left off the Tiverton to Dulverton road, B3222, just before Dulverton is reached, in Battleton. Hawkridge is clearly signposted again at Five Cross Way. Cars may be parked in the lane close to the church. These two loop walks are short, but take in a good variety of typical Exmoor countryside. Apart from the last lap of fairly steep hill-walking on returning to the village, the walk is not particularly strenuous. The optional loop is on tracked, but open, moorland.

At the time of researching the first walk, a large herd of red deer were seen, running in Hollowcombe and Hawkridge Ridge Woods. This is a favourite hunting venue; the season finishes at the end of April.

Hawkridge is a tiny village high on an open hill, 1000 ft above sea level. The views are beautiful, but the wind is fierce and rain, when it comes, slants aggressively. Choose a fine day for this walk. Teas are served in the village, but there is no pub.

Before starting the walk, visit the parish church of St Giles. The Norman doorway is a splendid link with the past history of the village; it is thought that the foundations of the church may be Saxon. In the yard outside is buried a great Exmoor huntsman, Ernest Bawden, of whom much has been written by Laurence Meynell in his book, 'Exmoor'.

Leaving the church on our right, we head down the lane indicated by the footpath sign to East Anstey.

After passing through two field gates a farm track leads to another sign, showing Dulverton 4¾ miles to the left and East Anstey Common to the right. Walking south east, this path goes into the woodland on the right, following a clear track that eventually descends to the valley floor and the lovely Danes Brook, a tributary of the river Barle. Stop, look, and listen for deer. In the spring, willow warblers sing here and buzzards cry above the trees.

A lyre-shaped footbridge spans the brook and, guided by yellow waymarks, the path leaves the woodland behind, emerging on the road. A footpath sign opposite indicates the track to the Ridge Road (East Anstey Common), but this walk turns right, following the road until a cattle grid is reached. This is Great Common, where a rough metalled track runs south west alongside a beech hedge. This is the optional loop, whereby the walk may be extended by a further 2 miles.

For this extra loop, follow the hedge and track until the Ridge Road is reached. The humps of West Anstey Barrows lie beside the path, Bronze Age burial mounds, reminding us that the Ridge Road was originally a prehistoric track. Views are quite spectacular, with Dartmoor to the south and the Cornish Moors lying south west, while all around the varying aspects of Exmoor show themselves on a clear day.

Follow the Ridge Road for a short distance. Various tracks lead off to the right, and it is easy to return to the Hawkridge road, but perhaps the simplest way is to follow the signed bridleway back from Anstey Gate, once again pausing to consider Froude Hancock's memorial stone en route. A total of 40 acres around this stone have been declared a memorial, dedicated to the pleasure of the public *ad infinitum*.

If the second loop is not taken, the road leads back to Hawkridge; notice the Two Moors Way coming down off the common, close to Slade Bridge. The Way is about 102 miles long and runs from Lynmouth on the North Devon Coast to Ivybridge in South Devon, traversing both Exmoor and Dartmoor, with very varied terrain.

A short way up the hill towards the village the Two Moors Way crosses a field on the right, a short cut back to the starting point of our walk. Head for the tree in the middle of the field, and then veer left to the iron gate in the far corner.

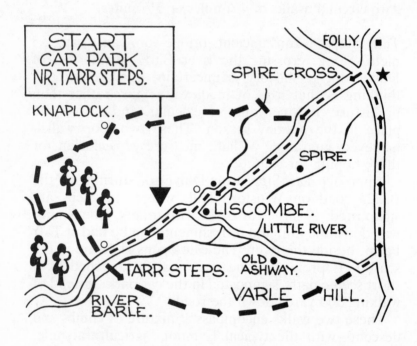

Tarr Steps

Two circular walks of 4¼ miles or 5½ miles.

Tarr Steps is an ancient bridge-cum-causeway, 55 metres long, crossing the river Barle north west of Dulverton. Its history is uncertain, but present day thinking is that it is of medieval origin, rather than prehistory. It is certainly spectacular, and a favourite place in the holiday season. These two loop walks, however, guarantee a slight measure of seclusion for those hoping for solitude.

Approach Tarr Steps from Dulverton, turning off the B3223 road on Winsford Hill, where the steps are signposted. A large car park, with toilets, stands midway down the hill, and refreshments can be had at Tarr Farm, beside the river. The cafe opens at 11 am in the season. If preferred, the river may be reached by a short scenic path, signposted in the car park, instead of walking 300 yards down the road.

These two walks encompass a mixture of climbs and descents with the typical Exmoor 'agricultural mile' putting the walker on his or her mettle. There is also some level walking, both on moorland and river paths. The routes are waymarked by the familiar yellow signs of the Exmoor National Park.

As an alternative to these walks, it is possible to take an easy, pleasant circular stroll of 1½ miles, starting on one side of the river at the steps and returning on the other. This is clearly signposted, and is made possible by 'permitted paths.'

For the first loop walk, leave the causeway and turn left, crossing the feeder stream by the small wooden footbridge, and then following the sign to Winsford via Summerway. A narrow, rough lane climbs the hill, with waymarks along the track.

From the top of Varle Hill – a good excuse to stop and catch one's breath! – the views are superb, with the wooded slopes above the river unfolding in varying shades of green and brown. In summer the birdlife is worth noting: buzzards, hawks, stonechats and larks abound.

Follow the path until it emerges close to a cattle grid. Continue along the road towards the B3223, and turn left. From here to the next turn – at Spire Cross – you can walk across open moorland, following the road.

Set back from Spire Cross and sheltered by a stone-built hut, stands the famous Caratacus Stone, an inscribed stone of the Dark Ages, thought to be a memorial to a kinsman of the British king of that name. Said to be the site of legendary treasure, this stone still retains its mystery. In 1936 it was uprooted, and left lying on the ground.

Turn left at Spire Cross and head back towards Tarr Steps. The first loop returns to the river by the road, passing Liscombe Farm and completing just over 4 miles, but the second, longer loop now branches off the road by the cattle grid, following the sign, 'Tarr Steps via Knaplock'.

This old road is unmetalled and rough. In summer the flowers and the trees provide evocative memories of travel in former times. The way winds down through the entrance to Knaplock Farm and through the yard, where a sign points the way ahead. The sunken lane is muddy, even in dry weather, but this is a beautiful walk. The lane leads down beside a deep, ravine-like cleft, waymarks indicating the way to the Barle and its sloping, tree-covered banks.

From the last sign Tarr Steps is merely a short stroll along the riverside, passing a debris-arresting cable stretched across the Barle, which failed to prevent damage to the causeway in 1979.

Tarr Steps has been breached many times in recent history. The middle sections were washed away in the winter of 1941–42, and following reconstruction more damage was sustained in the famous flood of 1952. Exmoor winters are harsh; how difficult to imagine this lovely, gentle place filled with roaring waters, causing even these solid stone slabs to give way.

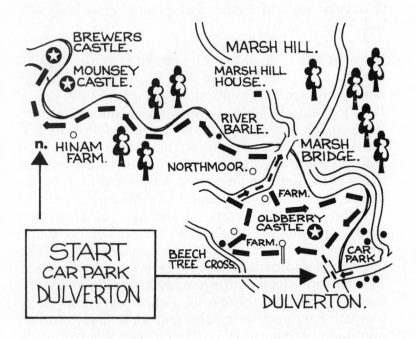

Dulverton

A circular walk of 3 miles and a longer river walk of 6 miles.

Dulverton is a small town by the river Barle. It is an excellent centre for exploring Exmoor and offers hotels, inns, refreshments and a good variety of shops. It is the main southern gateway to the Exmoor National Park, about 14 miles north of Tiverton, following first the A396 road then turning left on to the B3222. It is set among beautifully wooded valleys of the Barle and has many attractions for the visitor. Exmoor House, by the bridge, contains a very helpful information centre.

These two walks start on the side of Dulverton Bridge opposite the carpark. Waymarks sign the route, which passes some picturesque thatched cottages. Take the signed footpath to Beech Tree Cross, 1½ miles. This narrow, steep path is muddy after rain and is the hardest part of the entire walk. Follow waymarks as the footpath continues over fields and across a farm drive, eventually arriving at Beech Tree Cross, where a really magnificent tree fulfills the promise of its name.

The views on this first half of the loop are splendid, providing aerial scenes of Dulverton and the shining river Barle below. Once the muddy path has been achieved, there is a breath of exhilarating windswept air, as we pass the heights of Oldberry Castle, one of a group of Iron Age hill forts which defended the Barle nearly 2,000 years ago.

At Beech Tree Cross you have a choice of ways: the

road here runs back to Dulverton, or the farm road takes us on. The loop walk continues along this path, following yellow waymarks, passing the junction to Old Shute, and finally emerging on to the county road. Turn right and then, if you wish to return to Dulverton, turn right again where signposted, through the yard of Kennel Farm. This is an easy, riverside path of approximately 1 mile, returning to Dulverton Bridge.

For the second, longer walk, continue down the road to a point just before Marsh Bridge, where the path to Hawkridge, 3½ miles, is signposted. (If the first loop walk is *not* required, then Marsh Bridge can be reached by the riverside walk from Dulverton Bridge to Kennel Farm, picking up the Hawkridge sign from there).

From Marsh Bridge, follow the signs to Hawkridge and Tarr Steps along the side of the wide, beautiful river Barle. This is easy, uneventful walking with only occasional ups and downs. Watch for dippers and perhaps a heron. Ramsons and windflowers can be seen in spring, but the woodlands are lovely in all seasons.

Two miles from Marsh Bridge is Castle Bridge, spanning the tributary called the Danes Brook. Where the waters meet is an obviously defensible position, hence the two Iron Age hill forts on the wooded slopes on each side of the river here. Spare time for a breather on top of Brewer's Castle, beside the signed pathway that goes on to Tarr Steps. Mounsey Castle crowns the slope on the other side of the river.

From here – unless you are persuaded to continue to Tarr Steps – footsteps must be retraced to Marsh Bridge and the mile-long riverside footpath back to Dulverton, via the yard of Kennel Farm.

Bury

A circular walk of 4½ miles.

Bury is a picturesque hamlet with a ford and packhorse bridge in the Haddeo valley, 3 miles east of Dulverton, turning off the A396 road from Wheddon Cross to Exeter.

This part of Exmoor is not well known to visitors, although the creation of Wimbleball Lake Water Park in 1978 has opened up the area a little. The water park lies very close to the furthest extent of these walks and it is possible to visit the dam, which is 1½ miles from Hartford by signposted footpath through woodland.

This loop walk from Bury contains easy riverside paths, some woodland climbs and at least one excellent example of the true Devon green lane, used by man and beast for many centuries before the coming of the car.

The starting point is the road by the church in Bury marked with a 'No Through' sign – cars may be parked at convenient places in the village. This lane continues as a path and is signposted 'Louisa Gate 1 mile', to the left, and 'Bridleway to Hartford 2 miles', straight on.

This is very beautiful, lush country, with a profusion of woodland and hedgerows. The broad path is called Lady Harriet Acland's Drive and passes water meadows stretching down to the winding river. Bird life is undisturbed and ferns and flowers should please any botanist.

The path climbs gently as it continues and the true

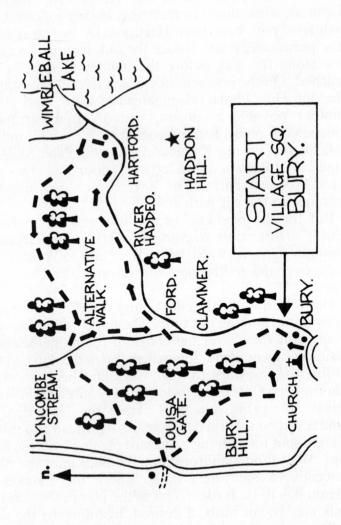

WIMBLEBALL LAKE

HARTFORD.

HADDON HILL.

RIVER HADDEO.

START
VILLAGE SQ.
BURY.

ALTERNATIVE WALK.

FORD.

CLAMMER.

BURY.

CHURCH.

LYNCOMBE STREAM.

LOUISA GATE.

BURY HILL.

n.

beauty of the valley can be seen. In spring and autumn the colours are at their best. The next footpath sign indicates the point where the return loop may, if required, come down to the river, having followed the high level path back from Hartford. Do not stray from this 'permissive path'. Notice the old, overgrown quarries along the way before the hamlet of Hartford is reached. On the opposite side of the river, bare-topped Haddon Hill, 1160 ft, dominates the scene, and offers another possible excursion, with its free car park, toilets, view point, and signposted walk to the Wimbleball Dam. (To reach Haddon Hill, take the Skilgate road out of Bury and turn left at the four-way cross just after Frogwell Farm. The next corner provides the entrance to the car park.)

But for the moment we are still walking to Hartford . . . Here, close to cottages at Hiccombe Green, a footpath signs the way back to Bury and to Wimbleball Lake over the footbridge, and through the trees, 1½ miles.

Our return walk takes the Louisa Gate track, a steep, stony path climbing out of the sheltered valley into the wind, with views over the hedge of rolling fields alternating with woodland, into which the path soon climbs, curling ever upward through oaks and beeches, with whortleberry bushes growing thickly among the tree trunks. In spring, bluebells carpet the ground. The wind, even on a warm day, screams overhead and this is a likely spot for sighting a buzzard planing over the tree tops. Wild rhododendrons now shoulder in as the path descends to the forest floor, where the Lyncombe stream has to be forded. This is the point at which the walk may be cut short, if desired, by following the sign to Bury along the river bank, retracing our outgoing steps.

The Louisa Gate path climbs again, becoming muddy

in places. Soon it emerges on the Dulverton to Brompton Regis road, opposite Barlynch woods, now a wild animal sanctuary created by the League of Anti-Cruelty Society.

There is a three-way footpath sign here; we dive into a broad drive along the top of the woodland and into a green lane hedged with beech. A field gate lower down affords a lovely view of patchwork fields, with Bury hiding in the valley below. This is a typical Devon sunken lane, with earthy banks and stony bottom, returning us to the point where the walk started.

The nearest opportunity for refreshments is Cowlings information centre and picnic area, sited on the western side of Wimbleball Lake, and easily reached from Brompton Regis. From this centre a nature trail and various waymarked paths around the lake may be followed.

Luxborough

Two circular walks, 3 miles plus an extension of 1 mile.

The small village of Luxborough, in the Brendon Hills, is best reached by turning left at Raleigh's Cross, roughly halfway on the B3190 road from Bampton to Watchet or by taking the Timberscombe turning on the A396 road from Dunster to Tiverton.

Luxborough is a divided village: the church and nearby school stand at the top of a hill, while Kingsbridge, more familiarly known as Pool Town, lies nearly a mile away, down in the valley where the little Washford river rattles along beside the road.

Pool Town is the starting point for these two loop walks which are fairly short but interesting and beautiful, taking in moorland and forest, with only one steep pull-up at the start of the walk.

The Royal Oak Inn, at the start of the walk, is a gem of a country pub, quiet and self-contained, its old oak settles, uneven flagstone floor and dim lighting capturing the imagination of any walker who calls in for a drink or a bar snack either before or after these walks.

A little way above the inn the road divides and the starting point is the convenient grass verge on the Rodhuish road close to a cottage, at 'Perley Ford', the foot of an old quarry. A public footpath sign marks the way to Dunster, 5 miles, and this is the track to follow. Go up the steep, rough path climbing Monkham Hill, following blue waymarks. Listen for the laugh of the green woodpecker and perhaps the call of a hunting

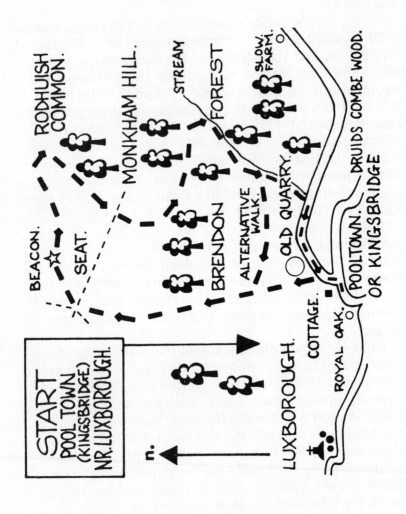

START
POOL TOWN
(KINGSBRIDGE)
NR. LUXBOROUGH.

BEACON.

RODHUISH
COMMON.

SEAT.

MONKHAM HILL.

STREAM

FOREST

BRENDON

ALTERNATIVE
WALK.

SLOW.
FARM.

OLD QUARRY.

POOLTOWN.
OR KINGSBRIDGE

DRUIDS COMBE WOOD.

COTTAGE.

ROYAL OAK.

LUXBOROUGH.

n.

buzzard in the deep valley to the left. There are great brown ant heaps in the woods, with ants foraging all over the path. Pause for breath occasionally and enjoy the views.

At the top of Perley Combe there is a five-way point with marked signs – Timberscombe left, Dunster straight on and then left, and Rodhuish right. Notice the rather dilapidated sign saying Bella's Lane and avoid resting on a rickety seat opposite. Withycombe Common lies to the right and we climb to the trig. point (the Beacon) at 1248 ft, where there are some really spectacular views to be seen. The Welsh mountains are hazy in the distance beyond Blue Anchor Bay, where the environs of Minehead can just be made out. Looking east you can see Hinckley Point at the foot of the Quantock Hills, and the Mendip Hills beyond.

Follow the track passing the trig. point through heather and springy turf and note the handsome contrast of the dark line of moorland forming a natural frame for a new picture of patchwork farmland in the valley beneath. Cuckoos sing here in late May, perhaps fooling the busy meadow pipits that abound everywhere.

Continue down this track until the paths unite. Turn right and right again, now walking parallel to a strip of woodland edging a beautiful grassed ride. You may see deer droppings here. There are two small pools of water around which you must pick your way, avoiding the boggy areas. When the ride meets the forestry road again turn left and then immediately right. It's downhill all the way now, following the rough path back towards Luxborough. Bird life here is varied and interesting: listen for stonechats, willow warblers and blackcaps in May and June. At the time of walking, a fox was flushed out of the rows of new planting on the left of the path, while along a shady little woodland path deer were seen grazing. A pair of ravens soared and called overhead.

Some way down this forest track a grassy path leads off to the right, which joins up with the steep footpath at the start of the walk. This completes the first loop, but an extra mile may be added on by continuing down the forest road, turning right after a short while through trees down a smaller track, and reaching a four-way crossing of forest tracks. Go straight on. Now this path becomes metalled in places, and is quite lovely, following a tumbling stream on the left, with great splashes of yellow broom lighting up the mixed planting above.

Follow the narrow road, eventually turning right and emerging, via a gateway on to the Rodhuish road. There is an antiquated signpost which indicates 'New Road'. Turn right here and return the short distance to the start of the walk at Perley Ford. If by any chance you wish to lengthen this last loop, the forest tracks continue through the woodland with frequent paths leading down to the Rodhuish road, further on from Perley Ford.

Horner Water

Two circular walks of 5½ miles.

Horner, approximately 4 miles from Porlock, is a delightful hamlet nestling in magnificent woodland at the foot of Dunkery Hill. It can be the excellent centre piece of a riverside walk of 5½ miles, starting at the wooded hairpin bend of Ley Hill, also approximately 4 miles distance from Porlock, towards Exford. Cars may be parked on the verge of the road at Pool Bridge, where a sign indicates the path to Horner, 2¼ miles. The Horner Water twists and turns through beautiful, but recently storm-damaged trees. Nesting boxes are in evidence in this National Trust woodland, and at the time of researching a pair of pied flycatchers delayed the progress of the walk. Dippers and grey wagtails haunt the grey boulders by the river. Several small, narrow footbridges span the water and there are plenty of opportunities to explore other woodland paths, if desired. Deer tracks can often be seen in the soft earth and the walker should watch for the deer themselves in the early morning or evening.

Eventually the Horner Water swings due north, arriving in Horner, a hamlet of farm and cottages, with an old millhouse currently being restored; obviously Horner was the hub of a network of medieval bridle-ways. Tea and coffee and light lunches are available during the summer season. Horses may be hired and there is an attractive but unobtrusive gift shop.

This is a lovely place, nestling in the vast surrounding

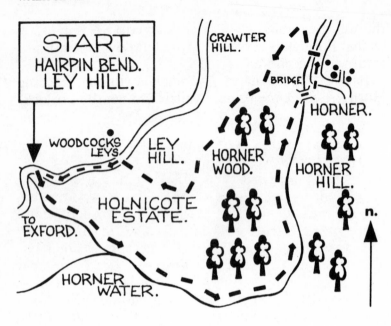

woodland, with a view of sombre Dunkery Hill as a backdrop in the distance.

There is a large free car park with toilets. Leaving the car park behind, turn off the road nearly opposite a pair of attractive stone cottages and cross the small, cobbled packhorse bridge to take the alternative return loop to Pool Bridge. Beyond the bridge turn right, turning sharp left some 20 yards further on. Follow the clearly defined rough, uphill path, called Granny's Ride, which climbs gradually to the top of the woods. There are some wonderful old trees. Look for an enormous oak, and consider all who have passed this way over the centuries.

At Horner Gate turn right and proceed along Flora's Ride which climbs Ley Hill to emerge on the road at the top. Sea gulls cry constantly overhead, reminding us that Porlock is very near. Turn left down the hill and return to the parked car.

If you dawdle in the woodland without reaching Horner, refreshments are available in nearby Porlock.

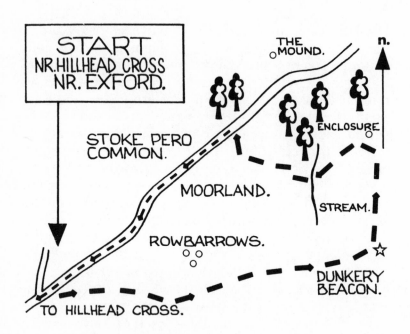

Dunkery Beacon

Two circular walks of 4 miles or 5¼ miles.

Dunkery Beacon stands 1705 ft above sea level and is the highest point on Exmoor. It commands wonderful, panoramic views and is therefore full of interest for the walker. Although easy enough to approach from the road at Dunkery Gate, at the eastern end of the long ridge, the beacon affords far more satisfaction if included in a longer walk. These two loops of easy walking offer alternative routes, both starting at the western edge of the ridge which the beacon crowns.

Approaching from Hillhead Cross – 3 miles along the Porlock road out of Exford – cars may be parked on the verge where the next fork, signed Stoke Pero, occurs. There is an obvious track here that goes straight to the beacon. There is also a bridleway on the ridge itself, passing Great and Little Rowbarrows – Bronze Age tumuli, so a choice may be made, but in either case Dunkery Beacon, 2 miles away, is the target.

Views crowd in from all sides. It is said that 15 counties may be seen on a fine day. The AA direction dial is a great help in naming the various landmarks set out below. Curlews may be heard here and deer roam freely in the early morning and late evening.

If wished the return journey can be made along the ridge, as the views are good enough to hold the interest going back, but a longer and really lovely loop can be made by walking due north from the beacon, heading for the distant sea, down the heathery hillside and exploring the hillslope camp of Sweetworthy, which lies just beyond the line of beech trees where the path joins a track running westward.

The old Iron Age camp lies in ruins amid the bracken. It is banked up on the south western side and dotted with birch and rowan trees. Overgrown and historically forgotten, it still retains an evocative atmosphere. It is best visited on a wild day, when mist hangs on the hillside and imagination may run riot.

From Sweetworthy, follow the track left, dipping down into a little combe with a spring. From here the track continues over Goosemoor Common, very soon reaching the road that crosses Stoke Pero common. Turn left and follow the gentle ups-and-downs until the starting point of the walk is reached.

There are no refreshment places nearer than Exford or Wheddon Cross.

Brendon Common

A circular walk of 6 miles.

This is a popular area for walkers and many paths and bridleways over the common are clearly waymarked. The view of the Chains, to the west, is magnificent. Cars may be parked off the road just beyond Dry Bridge, on the B3223 road from Simonsbath to Lynton, or, if the nearby memorial stone is to be visited, there is a car park sited close to it. The stone commemorates the death of an officer in the Second World War who died protecting his comrades in an accident.

At Dry Bridge a footpath points the way ahead – Rockford via Shilstone, 1¾ miles. This loop walk of approximately 6 miles which offers an alternative return route, is an easy ramble over moorland, through woods and along river paths. It is not strenuous walking and all one's energy and attention can be concentrated on the surroundings and scenery.

The signposted track passes the trig. point on Shilstone Hill, due north, and eventually slopes down over moorland to cross a small, negotiable stream at Shilstone Farm. Red marks clearly indicate the path through this well-kept farm with its attractive, warm stonework and mellow atmosphere of age.

Having left the farm behind, follow the lane, left, until a sign on the right indicates the way to Rockford. This woodland path is steep and inclined to be slippery, and in winter is awkward to negotiate. It joins the road in Rockford, running parallel to the powerful East Lyn

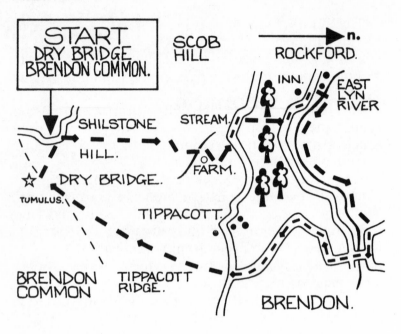

river below. Rockford is a tiny village, with Millslade House Hotel providing refreshments, riverside camping and 'Les Routiers' meals.

Following the road left, we retrace our steps by crossing the East Lyn by footbridge and then turning right for Brendon, the next port of call. This path is National Trust land and is clearly defined, following the river for 1 mile until it emerges into a field, close to an old packhorse bridge at Brendon.

A little further on is the road bridge, again crossing the river, and so arriving at the village green at Lee Ford Green, a crossing of four ways.

There is a post office in Brendon, a small village store, and the splendid Staghunters Inn. There is also a cafe for teas.

The return loop of this walk starts at Lee Ford Green, although a return to Rockford may be made by continuing along the road and linking up with the woodland path, returning to Brendon Common by way of Shilstone Farm again.

The route from Lee Ford Green carries on up the road signed to Tippacott. Cross Lane affords some excellent views of the village of Brendon below and its surrounding countryside. At Cross Gate, on the edge of the moor again, the way is signed due south to Brendon Common, 1½ miles. After ½ mile it joins a lower bridleway, coming in from the Doone Valley, and then forks right to rejoin the B3223 road at Dry Bridge, having passed by a large, humpy tumulus en route.

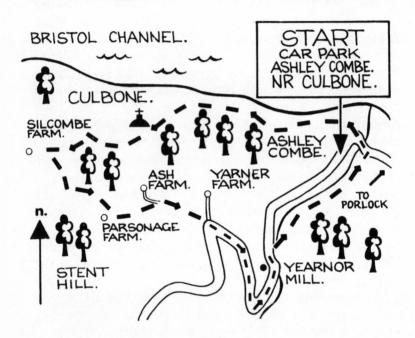

Culbone

A circular walk of 5 miles.

The coastal path is open, but prone to landslides, so walkers should check that it is accessible before starting out.

Culbone church is famed as the smallest parish church in England. It lies in a wooded combe, reached only by footpath and farm road, and provides the centre of a fascinating walk with plenty of ups and downs. However, for those who only wish to visit the church, it is pleasant enough to return to the starting point by retracing one's steps along the coastal path. As the coastal path is considered dangerous by the Exmoor National Park, due to erosion, it is taken entirely at the walker's own risk.

We start this walk at Ashley Combe Toll Gate, just outside the hamlet of Porlock Weir. At the harbour there are refreshment places, hotels and toilets. There is also a car park. There is another car park at Ashley Combe Toll Gate, reached by taking the Worthy road from Porlock Weir.

A signposted footpath which was open at the time of researching this walk, indicates the way to Culbone through coastal woodlands. Initially the walk is easy, a gently sloping path, with seats provided at regular intervals. The views are splendid, with the Welsh coast not far away. If the loop walk is continued after reaching Culbone, the going becomes a little harder, but cannot be described as difficult. It ends in a downhill slope along metalled roads, back to the car park.

Culbone Combe was once a small hamlet on a pack-horse route. Charcoal-burners and a colony of tanners lived and worked here, supposedly originating from a group of French prisoners-of-war sent to the combe in the early 18th century. And generation after generation of churchgoers found their way through the woods every Sunday to worship at the little church.

In recent years a working pottery was a great source of attraction to visitors but is no longer in existence. The church dates back to the 13th century and is full of atmosphere. The churchyard boasts a 15th century cross-base.

If the woodland path is retraced back to Ashley Combe Toll Gate, the remaining distance is a mere 1¼ miles. The loop walk, however, continues up through the combe, climbing the wood and emerging as a secondary road just below the entrance to Silcombe Farm. Turn left here, following the bends and hills back towards the Toll Gate, passing attractive Parsonage Farm and the entrance drives to Ash and Yarner Farms.

The woodlands are very fine, with flowers and wild life taking advantage of the excellent habitat. At the time of researching, the bridleway that turns off the road to the right, into the woods just above Yearnor Mill on the other side of the tumbling stream rushing down the combe, was damaged by fallen trees. If repaired and intact, it is a pleasant, alternative path, and emerges onto the road a few yards below the Toll Gate car park.

Malmsmead

Two circular walks of 3 miles or 6 miles.

These two loop walks are centred around the small, lovely hamlet of Malmsmead, the hub of the legendary Doone country written about by R.D. Blackmore in his novel 'Lorna Doone'. The first, shorter loop of 3 miles is over farmland, along a riverside path and on a quiet country road. The longer loop of 6 miles is initially along a riverside path, branching off through a solitary combe which climbs into moorland, and returning by a metalled road for a short distance. Both are moderately easy walking.

Malmsmead is most easily reached by turning off the A39 road from Porlock to Lynton, or from the A39 from Lynton to Blackmore Gate, approaching via the attractive village of Brendon. There is a large car park at Malmsmead with public conveniences, and many opportunities for refreshments at a picnic bar and local farmhouses.

The first loop takes the path to the Doone Valley, signposted some 300 yards along the road heading south from Lorna Doone Farm. When the footbridge over the river, close to Cloud Farm, is reached, a short loop may be made by crossing the bridge and following the track clearly marked to Oare church.

This is an evocative little church with simple box pews, and R.D. Blackmore's memorial tablet reminding the visitor that this was the setting he chose for the shooting of the heroine of his book, Lorna Doone, at her wedding to John Ridd.

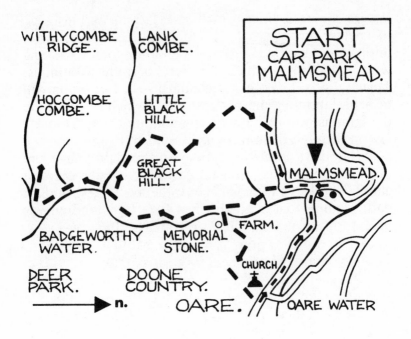

From Oare the road to Malmsmead is signposted and is a pleasant walk with a fresh view of the packhorse bridge and the ford as one arrives back at the starting point. In spring, wild mimulus crowns the grey boulders of the stream with glorious yellow blossom.

For the longer loop of 6 miles, follow the clear, riverside path opposite Cloud Farm down Badgeworthy Water, passing another handsome memorial to R.D. Blackmore and arriving, after 2 miles, at Hoccombe Combe, which is supposedly the site of the original Doone Valley. The views from this beautiful walk are many and varied, and the lower part of the valley, although visited by numerous tourists, still retains the solitude of the typical Exmoor scene.

Having explored Hoccombe Combe and the bumps and mounds of the deserted medieval village which inspire romantic images of Carver Doone and his gang of lawless men, turn back along Badgeworthy Water until Lank Combe is reached – another combe running west, and along which the return route continues. Turning into the combe, a smooth rock formation will be seen, about 30 metres upstream, which is said to be the famous water slide written about in 'Lorna Doone'. Go on through this lovely, solitary combe until you see a spasmodic line of thorn trees to the right. Take the obvious uphill track after the last tree and climb, via a gate at the top of the hill. Here the track joins a clear path leading to the road, then goes right and curves back to Malmsmead and a welcome cup of tea.

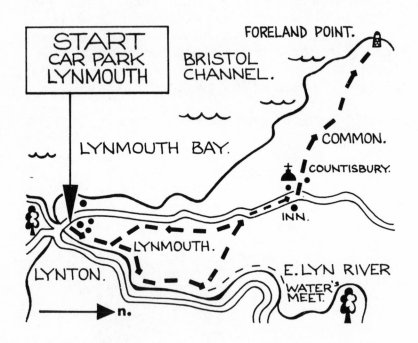

Lynmouth

Two circular walks of 4 miles or 1½ miles.

At Lynmouth there is a big car park by the bridge, which is the start of these two short loops. One is a riverside walk with a fairly steep climb through woodland, and the other is a short cliff walk. Lynmouth is busy in the tourist season and has many cafes and hotels. There is also an Exmoor National Park information centre.

From the car park, walk up Tors Road, following signs to Watersmeet. This is a good, safe path through beautiful National Trust woodland, easily walked beside the tumultuous East Lyn river. Look for the dipper, often seen on boulders in the river – a dark brown bird with a white bib. Its party tricks are to 'dip' and also to walk on the river-bed. When startled, it flies a low, straight-as-a-die path, hiding behind boulders until the human intruder has gone.

This riverside path winds between high, ravine-like slopes of oak trees. Jays scream, herons fish, and in the early spring there are primroses, ferns and budding bluebells in profusion. Yet the river itself is an awe-inspiring force with its constant crash of white water pounding the huge stones: a vivid reminder of the terrible 1952 flood disaster, when Exmoor's overflowing massed streams churned down this gorge, sweeping away much of Lynmouth in their wake.

On the opposite side of the river, Middleham Gardens are a fascinating reminder of the tragedy, ten cottages being destroyed by the flood. They stood beside an ancient packhorse route, and to mark their passing the cottage gardens are being replanted and opened to the public. Woodside Bridge enables walkers to visit these delightful gardens.

Having passed Woodside Bridge, the sign to Arnold's Linhay Path indicates the way to Countisbury, the furthest point of this loop walk, while the riverside path continues on to Watersmeet, the confluence of the Farley Water, the Hoar Oak Water and the East Lyn river. Perhaps you may decide to walk there on another occasion – Watersmeet House, with its restaurant and shop, is open from April to the end of October. It is owned by the National Trust, as is the entire Watersmeet estate, which has been designated a Site of Special Scientific Interest.

Arnold's Linhay Path is a reminder of a 19th century carter who pastured his ponies, donkeys and mules beside the Linhay where he lived. This path was probably the original road from Lynmouth to Countisbury.

Before you reach the top of the hill, look down through the trees and see Watersmeet House before indulging in the other spectacular panoramic views which abound here.

Countisbury is a small hamlet with a few cottages, a church, and an old coaching inn now called the Exmoor Sandpiper Inn. It is a hotel, offering bar food as well. Originally called The Blue Ball, some years ago it became The Blue Boar. Names change with owners, it appears, and once again it has been rechristened.

Opposite the inn a road to the left leads to the church and also to The Foreland. Beside the church the footpath passes along a grassy track on to the common. Here are wonderful cliff views and a signed track to The Foreland lighthouse. The cliff edges are high and steep – indeed, some of the highest in the country. If you don't like heights, or if the wind is dangerous, rest on the seat provided before returning past the church and the inn, taking the same footpath over the stile where the walk first emerged on Countisbury Hill.

At the sign 'Footpath to Lynmouth, 1¼ miles' take the higher track, which is uneventful but beautiful, winding along at the top of the wooded gorge of the East Lyn river. Seagulls and perhaps a raven soar in the heights and the views are breathtaking.

The path, 'Sparrows' Walk', descends in a series of zigzags which are easily negotiated, until the lower riverside path is reached, with Lynmouth only a short distance away.

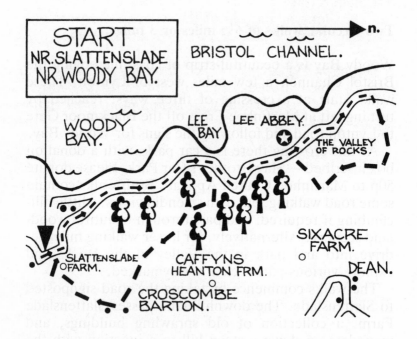

START
NR. SLATTENSLADE
NR. WOODY BAY.

BRISTOL CHANNEL.

n.

WOODY BAY.

LEE BAY

LEE ABBEY.

THE VALLEY OF ROCKS.

SLATTENSLADE FARM.

CAFFYNS HEANTON FRM.

SIXACRE FARM.

DEAN.

CROSCOMBE BARTON.

Woody Bay

Two circular walks of 6½ miles or 3 miles.

Woody Bay is a beautiful strip of coastline edging the Bristol Channel, a few miles west of Lynton. These walks start at a crossing of three ways, reached by turning left at Martinhoe Cross off the Blackmoor Gate to Lynton road and following the signs for Woody Bay.

At this crossing there is a car park, with a donation box inscribed – 'May Brother's Car Park. Please donate 50p to Martinhoe Church Appeal'. Both walks contain some road walking, but with splendid views, a little hill-climbing if required, and pass through beautiful woodland scenery. Alternatively, for lesser walking mileage, drive into and park in the Valley of the Rocks and explore various paths, clearly waymarked.

The walks commence by taking the road signposted to Slattenslade. The downhill lane passes Slattenslade Farm, a collection of old sprawling buildings, and meanders on down a steep hill to a junction with the road to Lynton. The views through the trees are magnificent, while the song of the sea is insistent background music. In mist this is a magical journey, with snatches of scenic beauty suddenly revealed and then again quickly hidden, as clouds move to and fro above. This lower road is part of the Somerset and North Devon coast path.

On a clear day the Welsh coast may be seen. Paths through the woods, to the right, are inviting, and the amazing construction of the accompanying drystone walls adds extra charm to the walk. The shorter loop now turns into the woods where Bonhill Cottages are signed through Crock Woods. This is a bridlepath to Croscombe Barton, waymarked in red.

The Barton is a fine old farm, at least 200 years old but with a history probably going back to the Norman Conquest. The path back to Slattenslade Farm is clearly marked, passing behind Croscombe Barton and then looping left. The way follows fields, keeping to hedge sides and walking due north west. In July the wild flowers beside these hedges are varied and beautiful; botanists in the party will thoroughly enjoy themselves. Watch out for redstarts, among a host of other better-known birds. The red waymark clearly indicates the path that finally emerges close to Slattenslade and the car park above.

For the longer walk, continue down the road, passing Lee Mouth Cottage, where the tea garden is open from Whitsun to October, but not on Sundays. Just beyond the Cottage is a car park, and the start of the toll road to Lynton, for which the charge at the time of writing is 30p per car.

Follow the hill up to Lee Abbey, a Victorian mansion in the mock-Gothic style, with some ruins of the original building. Lee Abbey is now a Christian community holiday and conference centre. Look for the 'White Lady' – details of which are given on a board beside the road; great imagination is needed to 'find the lady'!

The Valley of the Rocks – once thought to be a trapped lake – must definitely be explored and there are several signposted paths close to the car park. Our walk winds along the valley floor, with the monumental piles of Castle Rock and Rugged Jack towering above. Watch out for the little herd of wild goats that live here, often sheltering beneath Castle Rock.

Castle Rock Tea Gardens offer a licensed restaurant

with luncheons, cream teas, picnic food, gifts and off-licence. Our return path is signed just after the toilets, to the right of the road ahead. This path to Lynton climbs the hillside, soon reaching a path returning in the direction of Woody Bay. Turn right here, and follow the contour above Southcliff, running high above the valley. The views are stupendous and rewarding. Continue along the path, eventually descending by zigzags back to the road entering the valley.

The return walk now retraces our steps as far as the curve of the road beyond Lee Mouth Cottage, where we join the shorter walk, which followed the sign to Croscombe Barton. Alternatively, continue along the road, back to the parked car, shortening the walk by 1 mile.

Hunter's Inn

Two circular walks of 2 miles or 6 miles.

Hunter's Inn is reached by turning off the A39 road from Blackmoor Gate to Lynton and Lynmouth. It is clearly signposted and is approached by a very beautiful narrow, winding lane. This is one of the 'honey-pot' areas of Exmoor and so may be better avoided at the height of the tourist season. Refreshments are available at the hotel, which is a free house. There is a National Trust car park.

The first loop of these walks is on level ground, following the river Heddon on its mile-long sweep to the sea and back on the opposite side of the river. The walk is clearly signposted and the way is easy. There is a profusion of greenery and in summer the river runs through great clumps of balsam and montbretia. Above, the great screes climb to 700 ft and are awe-inspiring. The valley has been bought by the National Trust and is, indeed, an area of great beauty.

The beach at the end of the footpath is shingle, with large, smooth pebbles. The Bristol Channel is cold, but invigorating on a hot day; the ruined limekiln built into the rockface is a reminder of past busy days of lime importation from South Wales. Return to Hunter's Inn on the west side of the river.

The second loop is harder going and longer. Signposted to Martinhoe and Woody Bay, it starts at the same place as the river walk but very soon climbs uphill through woodland, following an old coach road until it

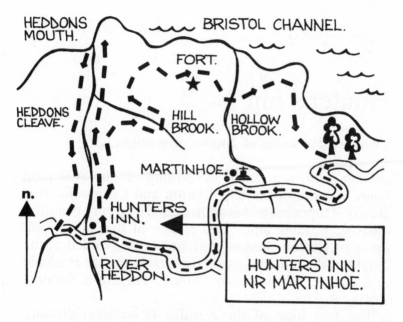

emerges on the bare hillside with spectacular drops and views all around. It is now a cliff walk, but not a dangerous one, as at all times the track is wide and unhindered. The views become breath-taking, particularly as the cleaves at Heddon's Mouth are left behind and the coastline stretches away to the east. The familiar shapes of the Valley of Rocks and Foreland Point can be recognised, while Wales, on a clear day, seems only a stone's throw away. Gulls wheel and scream, and the cliffs are almost too impressive for comfort.

This is a truly spectacular walk, with wild flowers growing in abundance beneath the sheltering slopes of the hillside, and a variety of bird and butterfly life. Two streams rush down to the sea; one, Hill Brook, at the first angle of the climbing path and the other, Hollow Brook, where the cliff path turns inward after following around the headland, now known as the Beacon, where once stood a Roman signal station. The path passes

57

through West Woody Bay Wood, badly damaged by blizzard in December, 1981, but now regenerating.

The path joins the Martinhoe Road, and we turn right, and again right at the three-way point signposted to Martinhoe. There are tumuli in the field to the left of the road, some of which were opened early this century; nothing of particular interest was found.

The Old Rectory, a country house hotel, stands close to St Martin's church and is a welcome stop on a warm day after such a demanding walk. The white-washed house holds considerable charm and the gardens are informal and lovely. A visit to the church, thought to date from the 13th century, is worthwhile. In the churchyard there are many tombs bearing the name of Ridd, a well-known name indeed in this part of the country.

The way back to Hunter's Inn branches right at Mannacott Lane Head, a crossing of four ways, and passes some old, picturesque buildings on the way down the hill, which in parts has a gradient of one in four.

There are many other walks in this area, and the National Trust has produced a helpful leaflet detailing them. It also mentions that it is actively controlling the unfortunate invasion of Himalayan knotweed to be seen, both in this valley, and on the Watersmeet estate.

Parracombe

A circular walk of 5 miles.

Parracombe is a small village on the slope of a hillside just below the Lynton to Barnstaple road. It is an ideal base for this walk of 5 miles over varied terrain of quiet country roads, farmland and open moorland, and the village itself offers great interest. Parracombe has a post office and one hotel, The Fox and Goose, as well as two churches.

This walk starts in the part of the village called Churchtown, where the 11th century church of St Petrock stands, just a stone's throw from the main road. Before reaching the church, there is rough parking on the road verge opposite the telephone kiosk; the carriageway must be kept clear.

In early spring the churchyard and its surroundings are white with snowdrops. This is a good time of the year for walking, with the sea air keen and bracing, and the winter colours and traceries still particularly beautiful.

St Petrock's church is closed during the winter months but may be visited by arrangement. It has a 12th century tower and an unchanged Georgian interior, complete with box pews.

To start the walk, head east, crossing the main road and following the signposted bridleway, which develops into a less stony footpath passing a newly built house before joining a metalled road, running south east through Parracombe Common.

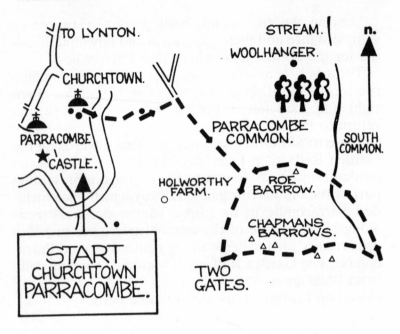

Turn right at the triangular piece of rough land and follow the road, bearing slightly right and uphill and arriving eventually at Two Gates – actually one iron gate, without a sign – and open moorland. Turn left, shutting the gate behind you, and climb the hill beside the hedge. The mounds of Chapman's Barrows dot the ground in an ascending line, burial places of a prehistoric race. The Negus stone is another, more modern, memorial recalling Robert Negus, who died in 1932, aged 17.

From this slope, looking south, the waters of Swincombe Reservoir can be seen. It is worth searching among the heather for the small standing stones on the ridge of this hill, just south west of the trig. point, (1574 ft) from which a superb view of the countryside opens up. Check your map for landmarks.

Leaving the trig. point, walk back (westwards) a short distance and then walk north and downhill, heading for the bottom field where Roe Barrow lies.

The track here joins once more with the metalled road running through Parracombe Common. Turn right and then left, retracing the outward path and return to Parracombe village.

Close to St Petrock's church is a sign advertising the Garden Railway at Fairview. This is a working model garden railway, its 16 mm to the ft gauge representing part of the old narrow gauge railway which once included Parracombe in its stops. The model track runs alongside a ¼ mile of the original track and provides opportunity for further walking centred around Parracombe. The Garden Railway is seasonal, opening daily from 10.00 am to 6.00 pm from Easter to October, and closed on Fridays. Teas are available here.

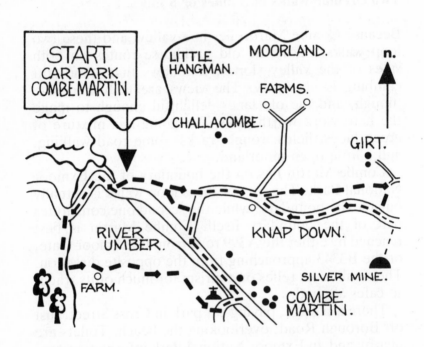

START
CAR PARK
COMBE MARTIN.

LITTLE
HANGMAN.

MOORLAND.

n.

FARMS.

CHALLACOMBE.

GIRT.

RIVER
UMBER.

KNAP DOWN.

SILVER MINE.

FARM.

COMBE
MARTIN.

Combe Martin

Two circular walks of 3 miles or 5 miles.

Because Combe Martin lies in a valley, and these two loop walks follow the old packhorse routes on both sides of the valley slopes, it follows that some stiff climbing is necessary. The views are truly majestic, though, and the old lanes delightful enough to make the hard work worthwhile. The going is a mixture of green lanes, fields, rough tracks, some road walking, and a little open moorland.

Combe Martin lies on the boundary of the Exmoor National Park. The first of these loop walks is actually outside the boundary, while the second one constitutes part of the boundary itself. Combe Martin is best reached by either the A399 road from Blackmoor Gate, or the B3343 approaching from the opposite direction. The small town relies on tourism for much of its trade, so cafes abound.

There is a large, paying car park in Cross Street, just off Borough Road, overlooking the beach. Toilets are nearby and an Exmoor National Park information centre is situated at the entrance to the car park. Enquire here for guided walks around the remains of the town's silver mines, and for a free copy of 'The Exmoor Visitor', which gives varied local information. The car park is the starting point for both these walks.

Follow the main road – Seaside Hill – keeping the beach on your right, and leaving the town. This road winds and climbs, and traffic is dangerous. The coastal path is signposted, also the car park for the Combe Martin museum. On the lefthand side of this road, at a steep bend, turn left; this is the start of a 30 mph area, and Furze Park is signed, beside Hillview Guest House. The lane dives down beside the main road, and a footpath sign is at once visible. This is a private road to Crackalands Farm, so dogs must be kept under control. Where the track divides, a yellow waymark on the telegraph pole shows the way. This is a pleasant, easy walk, the path travelling between high hedges at the foot of the sweep of hills known locally as The Seven Sisters. Footpath signs are clear and frequent. There is an abundance of flowers and trees, and at one point the path passes a cottage sheltered by a great wall of bamboo. The stream runs alongside until the path turns left, up a steep field. Catch your breath and pause to look back at the splendour of the scenery.

At the top of the field the way continues through a hunting gate. From here, head for telegraph wires ahead, and then take the clear track left, passing a handsome ruined stone gate-pillar, covered with golden and grey lichens. Footpath signs continue and soon the parish church comes into sight. Look across the valley ahead to one of the ruined silver mines that once contributed so largely to the world's supply of silver. Silver mining has been carried out in Combe Martin since 1290 and, along with strawberries, was the cause of the village's historical fame. The second loop of these walks can include a small extension to take a closer look at the old engine house chimney, if required.

The footpath, now a wider, more urban trackway, emerges at the parish church of St Peter ad Vincula. Turn left into Bowling Green Lane, beside the stream and the churchyard, and link up with High Street, at the right-hand side of the nearby car park. Head seawards now and, opposite the spectacular old building called The Pack of Cards, supposedly containing 52 windows to commemorate the cards with which a gambler won a fortune, turn right up Shute Lane, then left into West Challacombe Lane, following the sign for Hangman Hill. There are many beautiful, well-landscaped gardens among the houses and bungalows that border this road. Just beyond Five Turnings there is a multiple footpath sign. The end of this first loop turns left, down a dark, sloping smuggling lane, then left again, at Wayside, and by way of Rosea Bridge Lane returns to Borough Road and then right, to the car park, passing the Combe Martin Motor Cycle Collection as it does so.

The second loop begins at the multiple footpath sign, branching upwards towards Knap Down. This path soon rejoins the higher part of Shute Lane. This is a quiet country road with a keen incline. Seats are provided at frequent intervals and the views are beautiful, with the huge shoulders of the two Hangman Hills making breathtaking descents to the sea below, and the beach of Combe Martin to the left.

A little further up the hill is the entrance to the Silver Dale Nurseries tea gardens, open daily from 10 am to 6 pm, from Easter to October. This entrance lies at Netherton Cross and opposite the way to North and East Challacombe Farms. Just beyond the Cross a signposted footpath turns left, Knapdown Lane ½ mile, Great Hangman ½ mile. Knapdown Lane lies slightly outside the boundary of the Exmoor National Park and is a steep track, rough and often muddy, opening out onto a ridge with a bird's eye view of the imposing coastal countryside before us.

The bare heights of the Hangman Hills slope down into the valley at our feet, where the three Challacombe Farms are dotted. This is real beauty, with the old path we are walking passing beside gorse, and hedges which indicate earlier 19th century moorland enclosures. At the end of the path turn right onto the rough road called Girt Lane. Girt Lane soon rejoins Knap Down Road, and by turning right here we complete the second loop, descending to the car park via Rock Lane and Challacombe Lane.

An extra extension to this loop, if desired, turns left on rejoining Knap Down Road. A short way along, a footpath is signposted to High Street, turning right, into Corner Lane, and from here it is possible to get a good view of the old engine house chimney close to Silver Mines Farm. This is strictly private property, however, and there is no entry to the field in which the mine stands, its slag heap sprawled over with gorse. The fields near the mine are small, running in narrow strips down the hillside; some of these were allotments worked by miners.

The particular satisfaction of these two walks, on both sides of the river Umber valley, is that they follow old work and packhorse paths; many of the lanes are sunken, cut deep into rock and shady with abundant greenery. Spare a thought, as you walk, for the weary ponies and donkeys laden high with panniers, who also walked this way in the past.

Kinsford Gate

Two circular walks of 2¾ miles or 3½ miles.

For a complete change from other walks in this book, here is an easy circuit along quiet, moorland roads, high on the southernmost ridge of Exmoor, based on the ancient crossing of four ways at Kinsford Gate. It is best reached by taking the South Molton road from Simonsbath.

This elevated ridge walk is one of great scenic beauty and archaeological interest. On either side of this trackway Bronze Age man buried his dead, raising earthworks and stone barrows to their memory. The barrows have survived the erosion of weather and time and are now familiar landmarks for all who walk this way.

Approaching Kinsford Gate from Simonsbath, enjoy the impressive views as the road winds past the Fortescue memorial, with the river Barle meandering below in the valley. The Hon. Sir John William Fortescue, 1855–1939, was Historian of the British Army, but he spent much time at Simonsbath and no doubt drew upon his experiences there when he wrote, in 1887, his records of stag-hunting on Exmoor.

At Kinsford Gate, turn left and park on the grass verge. Both walks start here; the first, smaller loop of 2¾ miles crosses the South Molton road and heads north west up the road signposted to Challacombe. In the field to the left of the road are standing stones, tumuli and the famous Five Barrows. A sign to the effect that the stones are on private land, and that the public enter at their own risk, is soon reached.

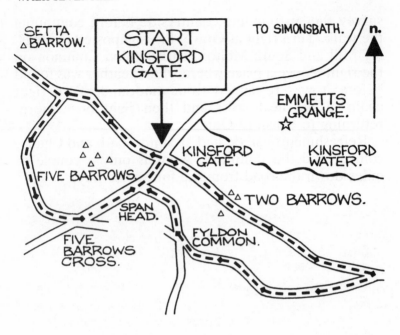

The loop turns left down a minor road, signposted unfit for motors, but it is worth continuing along the Challacombe road for a short distance to get a better view of Setta Barrow, which crowns the hilltop on the right. There are more tumuli on the left of the road, also.

Return via Five Barrows Cross to Kinsford Gate, having walked a complete circle. The views from all angles are magnificent, and it is worth waiting for a mist-free day before walking this circuit. The Bristol Channel lies due north, and Dartmoor raises its humps and bumps to the south.

At Kinsford Gate another loop may be walked in the opposite direction, following a right-handed route along the Sandyway and Molland road, pausing at the National Trust view point on the left at Two Barrows to survey the surrounding countryside before continuing the walk. Turn right at Gravel Pit, signposted to Heasley Mill and South Molton, with Fyldon Common on the right – once a place where white heather was found before it was reclaimed from moorland. Turn right again at the next cross and then right once more, returning to Kinsford Gate.

Refreshments can be had at Simonsbath and Challacombe, and the Poltimore Arms is only a couple of miles down the road from the four cross-way.

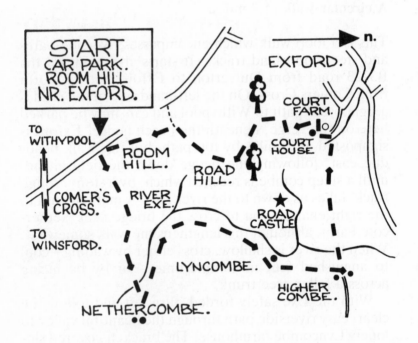

Room Hill, Exford

A circular walk of 5 miles.

This is a loop walk which encompasses riverside paths and steep moorland tracks. It starts at a point on the B3223 road from Dulverton to Exford not far north from Comers Cross. On the left-hand side of the road is a signposted path to Withypool and cars may be parked here on the verge, beneath the beech hedge. Exford is signposted as 2 miles by footpath, but this walk heads due east, following the hedge down the field ahead, until a steep combe is reached which, by a stony, rough track, takes us down to the river Exe. A marked path to the right enables you to cross the bridge near Nethercote Farm, although this lengthens the walk somewhat. When the river is shallow, cross either by wading – cool to anguished feet in summertime – or by balancing across a fallen tree trunk.

With the Exe safely forded, turn left and follow the clear, easy riverside path through the beautiful valley to lonely Lyncombe farmhouse. The bracken-covered slopes on the other side of the river are known locally as cleaves; they rise spectacularly from the water's edge.

Hidden away out of sight on the hilltop above Lyncombe, is Road Castle Camp, a small Iron Age hillside fort built 2500 years ago. Just before Lyncombe is reached, the camp can be seen on the opposite bank, its humpy turf banks showing up against the skyline. Pause at Lyncombe and look back; the view of the cleaves is truly magnificent, and a sight long to be remembered.

Beside Lyncombe a fine packhorse bridge heads in the direction of Road Castle Camp, but our way lies through the farmyard and on towards Higher Combe, from where a footpath takes us to Court Farm, by way of fields and a small forded stream.

At Court Farm it is only a step into Exford, where refreshments may be had. The return walk skirts the farmhouse, passing between hedges starred with sheepsbit scabious in high summer. The popping of ripe gorse pods provides a continuous fusillade, rowan trees are numerous and grasshoppers sing loudly.

Red dots indicate the way and the track bends uphill steeply. At the top of the field go left into the wooded valley. Raspberries are hidden in the hedge in season. Cross the feeder stream – a mere trickle in dry weather – and begin to climb. The way is rough and the going, in any weather, hard, but the views as you climb to the top of the field are wonderful. Dunkery and the Brendon Hills stretch before you, buzzards glide on their hunting circuits overhead, and this seems a good place to take a well-earned breather.

After reaching the ridge of beech trees, bear left over open, rough ground to a gate at the far corner of the field, and this path will return you to the starting point.

Simonsbath

A circular walk of 10¼ miles.

Although Simonsbath is the legendary heart of Exmoor, it is in reality a small hamlet providing a welcome oasis of green among the bare moorland surrounding it. It has two hotels and a cafe, all offering refreshment for the traveller, and is the hub of many lovely walks spreading out in all directions.

This walk involves some steep hillside scrambling, but is solitary and splendid.

Behind the Exmoor Forest Hotel there is a free car park with toilets. On the left hand side of the road, heading down to Simonsbath Bridge, there is a gate, which is the start of this walk. Red waymarks show the path to Landacre by Pickedstones, 5 miles, and yellow signs indicate the alternative path to Landacre via Cow Castle, 5¼ miles. Walking either way creates a useful loop, returning to the starting point. If a shorter walk is wanted, then take the yellow sign, which follows the river Barle, providing a most enjoyable stroll of any length required, returning the same way.

Choosing the red waymarks to Landacre (which is the longer walk), climb up through Birchwood Cleave. Recent gales caught the tops of many beech trees here and so the ground is littered with trunks and stumps, but new planting is filling up the spaces. The red waymarks head away from the river, passing through field gates and providing easy walking through several fields. Notice the low farm buildings of Winstitchen

Farm and imagine how the winter winds must rampage at times.

To the right, the lines of enfolding moorland on the opposite side of the river are beautiful. Very soon the path joins what clearly must have once been, from the thick wheel ruts, an old cart track. Probably this was originally the road to Withycombe, once used by farmers and stock, now preserved by walkers.

The path continues, following the cart tracks, en route for Pickedstones Farm. Just before the farm, look right for a wonderful view of the river below. Cow Castle, an Iron Age fort, stands at a sharp bend, the turf rampart enclosing it plainly visible from the vantage point of our walk. A smaller mound beside Cow Castle is known as The Calf. The path running behind the Castle is the return track to Simonsbath.

Red signs take us up the drive of Pickedstones Farm and into the second field gate on the right, by telegraph poles. Cross this field diagonally to a waymarked gate, and then on to scrubby moorland, signposted straight ahead.

Continue along this track until it converges with another turning sharply right, back on itself. This is the way back to Simonsbath, and part of the Two Moors Way. Look out for a herd of Exmoor ponies – one of three which graze these moorlands. True Exmoors are recognisable by their 'toad-eyes' and 'mealy noses', and these three herds are being closely managed in order to preserve the true strain.

Follow the yellow signs now, descending to the river, and looking back, left, to see Landacre Bridge, with its medieval five arches. The Two Moors Way crosses the river at a footbridge, but our walk stays on the east side of the Barle, passing beside a conifer plantation before reaching Cow Castle.

Heading for Simonsbath, the path passes beside the huge mound called Flexbarrow, dotted with dead trees, and beyond that are the ruins of the old iron mine, Wheal Eliza, in use from 1846 onwards. This is a lonely, spectacular place with wonderful views. Look out for buzzards, dippers, and perhaps a heron down on the river bank.

The footpath follows the river without event, returning to Simonsbath via Birchwood Cleave, our starting point.

Pinkworthy Pond
on The Chains

Circular walks of 3 miles, 4¼ miles, 7 miles and 9 miles.

The area of Exmoor known as The Chains offers the most arduous walks in this book. Here, in the steep valleys that fringe this central plateau, three rivers have their source, carrying life-giving fertility through bare moorland and hard-worked farmland. Those who have not walked on The Chains have not really experienced the true Exmoor. The walking is tussocky, often boggy, and there is some steep hill climbing. Proper footwear, weatherproof clothing and a map is essential. A compass can be helpful, as mist comes down fast and unexpectedly.

The last two walks detailed here should not be attempted in bad weather. Choose a suitable day, for they are satisfying and strenuous outings which will convey Exmoor's true qualities. No doubt walkers will agree that solitude and beauty are more than adequate compensations for wet feet and aching muscles.

Cars may be parked at Goat Hill, on the verge of the B3358 road from Simonsbath to Blackmoor Gate, or in the small parks on the road verges before reaching Goat Hill from Simonsbath.

The first walk suggested is an easy ramble of 3 miles, following the clear footpath signposted to Pinkworthy (pronounced Pinkery) Pond, and returning the same way. The track crosses fields below Pinkworthy Farm –

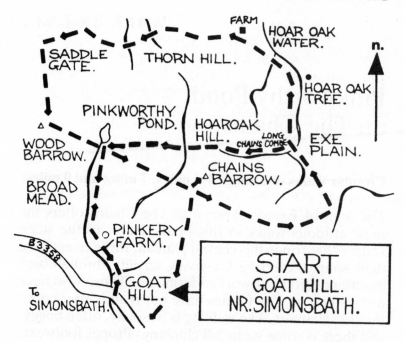

now Pinkworthy Outdoor Exploration Centre – and runs beside the infant river Barle until the dam of Pinkworthy Pond is reached.

John Knight built this dam in 1837, importing 200 Irish labourers to do so, but for what reason is not known. Perhaps the pond was meant to be an ornamental lake – or to provide power for Knight's many schemes destined to reclaim the moorland. It remains as a memorial to the man whose vision and determination made Exmoor what it is today.

The second walk from Pinkworthy turns right and follows the South Chains Wall for ¾ mile. The ground here is tussocky and uneven, boggy in wet weather. Beware of hidden, deep irrigation channels as you walk. They can be detected if you carefully look for the lighter green of the grass hiding them.

77

Larks sing here and perhaps a hare will start up at your feet. The shadows of clouds chase the sunlight over the moor in fast-moving shapes. Hawks hunt overhead and it is a source of delight to watch them hover, spying out their prey, before wheeling away into the wind. It is nearly always windy on The Chains, battering the walker with enthusiastic noise.

Take a detour to the Chains Barrow, which rises in solitary splendour on the left, crowned by the Ordnance Survey trig. point from which extensive views can be seen on a fine day. The height here is almost 1600 ft.

This second walk ends by returning to the Wall and continuing back to the B3358 via a bridlepath through easily-walked grazing land. This path emerges on the road just below the first of the car parks mentioned above, a pleasant round walk of just over 4 miles.

A longer and much harder walk of 9 miles, mostly over wet ground, with steep combes to negotiate, takes you straight on after visiting Chains Barrow, following the Wall for over another mile. Turn left, just short of Exe Head, where a clear track comes into this one. This is a part of the Two Moors Way, running through Dartmoor and into Exmoor, ending at Lynmouth. Head north east, to the combe that is already unfolding nearby. Walking becomes easier now.

Follow the path down into the sheltered valley of the Hoar Oak Water, crossing the stream where another small valley runs in from the west. This is beautiful Long Chains Combe, tucked beneath Hoar Oak Hill, a good spot for a rest after the energetic walking required to reach it. Mining remains abound here. Watch and listen for ravens. Wire-fenced Hoar Oak Tree can be seen at the end of the combe, on the opposite side of the stream.

The original Hoar Oak was planted here to mark the boundary of Exmoor Forest in 1300. In 1658 it fell down from old age and another tree was planted, to be blown down in 1916. This present tree is the latest in a very ancient tradition.

For the shorter walk of 7 miles, return to Long Chains Combe and walk due west across open moor for approximately 1 mile, to return to Pinkworthy Pond. A compass bearing should be taken here until the dam comes into view.

The really addicted moor-rambler, however, will doubtless prefer to go on past the Hoar Oak Tree, climbing left and following the county boundary. This is hard walking. The ruin of Hoar Oak Farm lies to the right, and the track leads down into another combe, then begins once more the breathtaking upward climb. The going becomes more difficult, with bog pulling at one's feet, and occasionally throwing up the blanched bones of past victims. Animals sometimes become 'stugged' and lose their lives. Spare a moment to survey the scene. Wales lies beyond the humpy coastal outline and Brendon Common sprawls away to the north east, with farmland spreading a gentler patchwork pattern in the valley below.

Continue following the dry stone wall. Ruckham Combe is steep and demanding, but after that the way back to Pinkworthy becomes easier. Follow the county boundary wall, which turns left at Saddle Gate – it is possible here to cut the corner, if desired – where a bridlepath returns, south, to Woodbarrow Gate. Here there is a choice of ways; the path straight on emerges on the B3358, ½ mile north east of Goat Hill, while the path to the left goes to Pinkworthy Pond and the returning track to the road where these walks started.